My Favorite Recipes

compiled by

_____

_____

_____

_____

date

_____

My Favorite
Recipes

**Capture your family's
favorite recipes and traditions**

Published by
FRP
P.O. Box 305142
Nashville, Tennessee 37230
1-800-358-0560

Copyright ©2006 by
FRP
Images ©StockFood and Dover Publications

ISBN: 0-87197-524-6

Manufactured in China
First Printing: 2006

Additional Cookbooks by **FRP**

Almost Homemade – Cake Mix Desserts
Quick & Easy Grilling – Over 100 Fast & Furious Timesaving Recipes
The Vintner's Table – Recipes from a Winery Chef

To order these and many other award-winning
community cookbooks go to:
www.cookbookmarketplace.com or
www.frpbooks.com
1-800-269-6839

Contents

Have you ever wanted to write your own cookbook? Do you wish you had one place to go to find all of your most cherished recipes? Now you can! Every family has its favorite recipes, traditions, and special memories. *My Favorite Recipes* makes it easy for you to preserve those family favorites in this easy-to-use recipe journal. Record your recipes to ensure they are not lost, and you will have a cookbook written by you that will be cherished for years to come.

There is room for over 150 recipes, with space for helpful hints, serving suggestions, or personal food memories on each page. In addition, for the user's convenience, a handy index has been included in the back of the book, so don't forget to keep it updated as you add new recipes.

Introduction

Another wonderful feature of *My Favorite Recipes* is the Recipe Finder Index—an index designed to record favorite recipes prepared from your favorite cookbooks. Simply write in the name of the recipe, the title of the cookbook, and the page number! No more searching through your entire cookbook collection to find the recipe that you used last month and that your family is asking for again.

Feel free to personalize your book by adding photos, personal stories of what a particular recipe means to you, or memories of family gatherings at mealtime. This is your opportunity to create what is sure to become a family heirloom.

Appetizers

appetizers

Recipe Name _____ Serves _____

Ingredients

Method

notes

appetizers

Recipe Name _____ Serves _____

Ingredients

_____ _____
_____ _____
_____ _____
_____ _____

Method

_____
_____
_____
_____
_____
_____

notes _____
_____
_____

appetizers

Recipe Name _____ Serves _____

Ingredients

_____ _____
_____ _____
_____ _____

Method

_____
_____
_____

notes _____
_____
_____

appetizers

Recipe Name _____ Serves _____

Ingredients

_____   _____
_____   _____
_____   _____
_____   _____
_____   _____
_____   _____
_____   _____
_____   _____
_____   _____

Method

_____
_____
_____
_____
_____
_____
_____
_____
_____
_____
_____
_____
_____
_____
_____
_____

notes
_____
_____

 *appetizers*

Recipe Name _____ Serves _____

Ingredients

_____   _____
_____   _____
_____   _____
_____   _____

Method

_____
_____
_____
_____
_____
_____

_____ *notes* _____
_____
_____

appetizers

Recipe Name _____ Serves _____

Ingredients

_____   _____
_____   _____
_____   _____

Method

_____
_____
_____
_____
_____

_____ *notes* _____
_____
_____

appetizers

Recipe Name _____ Serves _____

Ingredients

_____ _____

_____ _____

_____ _____

_____ _____

_____ _____

_____ _____

_____ _____

_____ _____

_____ _____

Method

_____

_____

_____

_____

_____

_____

_____

_____

_____

_____

_____

_____

_____

_____

_____

_____

_____

_____

notes _____

_____

 *appetizers*

Recipe Name _____ Serves _____

Ingredients

_____   _____
_____   _____
_____   _____
_____   _____

Method

_____
_____
_____
_____
_____
_____
_____
_____ *notes* _____
_____
_____

appetizers

Recipe Name _____ Serves _____

Ingredients

_____   _____
_____   _____
_____   _____
_____   _____

Method

_____
_____
_____
_____
_____ *notes* _____
_____
_____

 *appetizers*

Recipe Name _____ Serves _____

Ingredients

Method

notes

appetizers

Recipe Name _____ Serves _____

Ingredients
_____   _____
_____   _____
_____   _____
_____   _____

Method
_____
_____
_____
_____
_____
_____

notes
_____
_____

appetizers

Recipe Name _____ Serves _____

Ingredients
_____   _____
_____   _____
_____   _____
_____   _____

Method
_____
_____
_____
_____

notes
_____
_____

 *appetizers*

Recipe Name _____ Serves _____

Ingredients
_____   _____
_____   _____
_____   _____
_____   _____
_____   _____
_____   _____
_____   _____
_____   _____
_____   _____

Method
_____
_____
_____
_____
_____
_____
_____
_____
_____
_____
_____
_____
_____
_____
_____
_____
_____
_____

notes
_____
_____

 *appetizers*

Recipe Name _____ Serves _____

Ingredients

_____   _____
_____   _____
_____   _____
_____   _____

Method

_____
_____
_____
_____
_____
_____

notes

_____
_____

appetizers

Recipe Name _____ Serves _____

Ingredients

_____   _____
_____   _____
_____   _____
_____   _____

Method

_____
_____
_____
_____
_____

notes

_____
_____

 *appetizers*

Recipe Name _____ Serves _____

Ingredients

_____   _____
_____   _____
_____   _____
_____   _____
_____   _____
_____   _____
_____   _____
_____   _____
_____   _____

Method

_____
_____
_____
_____
_____
_____
_____
_____
_____
_____
_____
_____
_____
_____
_____
_____
_____

notes

_____
_____

 *appetizers*

Recipe Name _____ Serves _____

Ingredients
_____   _____
_____   _____
_____   _____
_____   _____

Method
_____
_____
_____
_____
_____
_____

_____ *notes* _____
_____
_____

appetizers

Recipe Name _____ Serves _____

Ingredients
_____   _____
_____   _____
_____   _____
_____   _____

Method
_____
_____
_____
_____
_____

_____ *notes* _____
_____
_____

 *appetizers*

Recipe Name _____ Serves _____

Ingredients

_____   _____
_____   _____
_____   _____
_____   _____
_____   _____
_____   _____
_____   _____
_____   _____
_____   _____

Method

_____
_____
_____
_____
_____
_____
_____
_____
_____
_____
_____
_____
_____
_____
_____
_____

notes

_____
_____

 *appetizers*

Recipe Name _____ Serves _____

Ingredients

Method

notes

appetizers

Recipe Name _____ Serves _____

Ingredients

Method

notes

appetizers

Recipe Name _____ Serves _____

Ingredients

_____   _____
_____   _____
_____   _____
_____   _____
_____   _____
_____   _____
_____   _____
_____   _____
_____   _____

Method

_____
_____
_____
_____
_____
_____
_____
_____
_____
_____
_____
_____
_____
_____
_____
_____
_____
_____

notes

Soups

 soups

Recipe Name _____ Serves _____

Ingredients
_____   _____
_____   _____
_____   _____
_____   _____
_____   _____
_____   _____
_____   _____
_____   _____
_____   _____

Method
_____
_____
_____
_____
_____
_____
_____
_____
_____
_____
_____
_____
_____
_____
_____
_____
_____
_____

notes
_____
_____

 *soups*

Recipe Name _____ Serves _____

Ingredients

_____   _____
_____   _____
_____   _____
_____   _____

Method

_____
_____
_____
_____
_____
_____

notes

_____
_____

soups

Recipe Name _____ Serves _____

Ingredients

_____   _____
_____   _____
_____   _____
_____   _____

Method

_____
_____
_____
_____
_____
_____

notes

_____
_____

 *soups*

Recipe Name _____ Serves _____

Ingredients

_____   _____
_____   _____
_____   _____
_____   _____
_____   _____
_____   _____
_____   _____
_____   _____

Method

_____
_____
_____
_____
_____
_____
_____
_____
_____
_____
_____
_____
_____
_____
_____
_____
_____
_____
_____

notes

_____
_____

 *soups*

Recipe Name _____ Serves _____

Ingredients

_____   _____
_____   _____
_____   _____
_____   _____

Method

_____
_____
_____
_____
_____
_____

notes

_____
_____

soups

Recipe Name _____ Serves _____

Ingredients

_____   _____
_____   _____
_____   _____
_____   _____

Method

_____
_____
_____
_____

notes

_____
_____

 *soups*

Recipe Name _____ Serves _____

Ingredients

_____   _____
_____   _____
_____   _____
_____   _____
_____   _____
_____   _____
_____   _____
_____   _____
_____   _____

Method

_____
_____
_____
_____
_____
_____
_____
_____
_____
_____
_____
_____
_____
_____
_____
_____
_____
_____
_____

notes
_____
_____

 *soups*

Recipe Name _____ Serves _____

Ingredients

_____   _____
_____   _____
_____   _____
_____   _____

Method

_____
_____
_____
_____
_____
_____
_____

notes
_____
_____

soups

Recipe Name _____ Serves _____

Ingredients

_____   _____
_____   _____
_____   _____
_____   _____

Method

_____
_____
_____
_____
_____
_____

notes
_____
_____

 *soups*

Recipe Name _____ Serves _____

Ingredients

Method

notes

 *soups*

Recipe Name _____ Serves _____

Ingredients

_____   _____
_____   _____
_____   _____
_____   _____

Method

_____
_____
_____
_____
_____
_____
_____

_____ *notes* _____
_____
_____

soups

Recipe Name _____ Serves _____

Ingredients

_____   _____
_____   _____
_____   _____
_____   _____

Method

_____
_____
_____
_____
_____

_____ *notes* _____
_____
_____

 *soups*

Recipe Name _____ Serves _____

Ingredients

_____   _____
_____   _____
_____   _____
_____   _____
_____   _____
_____   _____
_____   _____
_____   _____
_____   _____
_____   _____

Method

_____
_____
_____
_____
_____
_____
_____
_____
_____
_____
_____
_____
_____
_____
_____
_____
_____
_____

notes
_____
_____

Salads

 *salads*

Recipe Name _____ Serves _____

Ingredients

Method

notes

 *salads*

Recipe Name _____ Serves _____

Ingredients

_____   _____
_____   _____
_____   _____
_____   _____

Method

_____
_____
_____
_____
_____
_____
_____

notes

_____
_____

salads

Recipe Name _____ Serves _____

Ingredients

_____   _____
_____   _____
_____   _____
_____   _____

Method

_____
_____
_____
_____
_____
_____

notes

_____
_____

 *salads*

Recipe Name _____ Serves _____

Ingredients

_____ _____
_____ _____
_____ _____
_____ _____
_____ _____
_____ _____
_____ _____
_____ _____
_____ _____

Method

_____
_____
_____
_____
_____
_____
_____
_____
_____
_____
_____
_____
_____
_____
_____
_____
_____
_____
_____

notes

_____
_____

 *salads*

Recipe Name _____ Serves _____

Ingredients

_____   _____
_____   _____
_____   _____
_____   _____

Method

_____
_____
_____
_____
_____
_____

notes

_____
_____

salads

Recipe Name _____ Serves _____

Ingredients

_____   _____
_____   _____
_____   _____
_____   _____

Method

_____
_____
_____
_____
_____

notes

_____
_____

 *salads*

Recipe Name _____ Serves _____

Ingredients

_____   _____
_____   _____
_____   _____
_____   _____
_____   _____
_____   _____
_____   _____
_____   _____
_____   _____

Method

_____
_____
_____
_____
_____
_____
_____
_____
_____
_____
_____
_____
_____
_____
_____
_____
_____

notes
_____
_____

 *salads*

Recipe Name _____ Serves _____

Ingredients

_____ _____
_____ _____
_____ _____
_____ _____

Method

_____
_____
_____
_____
_____
_____

notes

_____
_____

salads

Recipe Name _____ Serves _____

Ingredients

_____ _____
_____ _____
_____ _____
_____ _____

Method

_____
_____
_____
_____
_____
_____

notes

_____
_____

 *salads*

Recipe Name _____ Serves _____

Ingredients

_____   _____
_____   _____
_____   _____
_____   _____
_____   _____
_____   _____
_____   _____
_____   _____

Method

_____
_____
_____
_____
_____
_____
_____
_____
_____
_____
_____
_____
_____
_____
_____
_____
_____

notes

_____
_____

 *salads*

Recipe Name _____ Serves _____

Ingredients

_____   _____
_____   _____
_____   _____
_____   _____

Method

_____
_____
_____
_____
_____
_____

notes

_____
_____

salads

Recipe Name _____ Serves _____

Ingredients

_____   _____
_____   _____
_____   _____
_____   _____

Method

_____
_____
_____
_____
_____

notes

_____
_____

 salads

Recipe Name _____ Serves _____

Ingredients

Method

notes

Meats

 *meats*

Recipe Name _____ Serves _____

Ingredients

_____   _____
_____   _____
_____   _____
_____   _____
_____   _____
_____   _____
_____   _____
_____   _____
_____   _____

Method

_____
_____
_____
_____
_____
_____
_____
_____
_____
_____
_____
_____
_____
_____
_____
_____
_____
_____

notes
_____
_____

 *meats*

Recipe Name _____ Serves _____

Ingredients

_____   _____
_____   _____
_____   _____
_____   _____

Method

_____
_____
_____
_____
_____
_____

notes
_____
_____

meats

Recipe Name _____ Serves _____

Ingredients

_____   _____
_____   _____
_____   _____

Method

_____
_____
_____
_____

notes
_____
_____

 *meats*

Recipe Name _____ Serves _____

Ingredients

Method

notes

 *meats*

Recipe Name _____ Serves _____

Ingredients

_____   _____
_____   _____
_____   _____
_____   _____

Method

_____
_____
_____
_____
_____
_____

notes

_____
_____

meats

Recipe Name _____ Serves _____

Ingredients

_____   _____
_____   _____
_____   _____
_____   _____

Method

_____
_____
_____
_____

notes

_____
_____

 *meats*

Recipe Name _____ Serves _____

Ingredients

Method

notes

 *meats*

Recipe Name _____ Serves _____

Ingredients

_____ _____
_____ _____
_____ _____
_____ _____

Method

_____
_____
_____
_____
_____
_____

notes

_____
_____

meats

Recipe Name _____ Serves _____

Ingredients

_____ _____
_____ _____
_____ _____
_____ _____

Method

_____
_____
_____
_____

notes

_____
_____

 meats

Recipe Name _____ Serves _____

Ingredients

_____   _____
_____   _____
_____   _____
_____   _____
_____   _____
_____   _____
_____   _____
_____   _____
_____   _____

Method

_____
_____
_____
_____
_____
_____
_____
_____
_____
_____
_____
_____
_____
_____
_____
_____
_____

notes

_____
_____

 *meats*

Recipe Name _____ Serves _____

Ingredients

_____   _____
_____   _____
_____   _____
_____   _____

Method

_____
_____
_____
_____
_____
_____

notes

_____
_____
_____

meats

Recipe Name _____ Serves _____

Ingredients

_____   _____
_____   _____
_____   _____
_____   _____

Method

_____
_____
_____
_____
_____

notes

_____
_____
_____

 *meats*

Recipe Name _____ Serves _____

Ingredients

_____   _____
_____   _____
_____   _____
_____   _____
_____   _____
_____   _____
_____   _____
_____   _____
_____   _____
_____   _____

Method

_____
_____
_____
_____
_____
_____
_____
_____
_____
_____
_____
_____
_____
_____
_____
_____
_____

notes
_____
_____

 *meats*

Recipe Name _____ Serves _____

Ingredients

_____   _____
_____   _____
_____   _____
_____   _____

Method

_____
_____
_____
_____
_____
_____

notes _____
_____
_____

meats

Recipe Name _____ Serves _____

Ingredients

_____   _____
_____   _____
_____   _____
_____   _____

Method

_____
_____
_____
_____
_____

notes _____
_____
_____

 meats

Recipe Name _____ Serves _____

Ingredients

_____   _____
_____   _____
_____   _____
_____   _____
_____   _____
_____   _____
_____   _____
_____   _____

Method

_____
_____
_____
_____
_____
_____
_____
_____
_____
_____
_____
_____
_____
_____
_____
_____

notes
_____
_____

 *meats*

Recipe Name _____ Serves _____

Ingredients

_____ _____
_____ _____
_____ _____
_____ _____

Method

_____
_____
_____
_____
_____
_____

notes

_____
_____

meats

Recipe Name _____ Serves _____

Ingredients

_____ _____
_____ _____
_____ _____
_____ _____

Method

_____
_____
_____
_____
_____

notes

_____
_____
_____

 *meats*

Recipe Name _____ **Serves** _____

Ingredients

_____   _____
_____   _____
_____   _____
_____   _____
_____   _____
_____   _____
_____   _____
_____   _____
_____   _____

Method

_____
_____
_____
_____
_____
_____
_____
_____
_____
_____
_____
_____
_____
_____
_____
_____

notes _____
_____

Poultry

 *poultry*

Recipe Name _____ Serves _____

Ingredients

Method

notes

 *poultry*

Recipe Name _____ Serves _____

Ingredients

_____   _____
_____   _____
_____   _____
_____   _____

Method

_____
_____
_____
_____
_____
_____

notes

_____
_____

poultry

Recipe Name _____ Serves _____

Ingredients

_____   _____
_____   _____
_____   _____

Method

_____
_____
_____
_____
_____

notes

_____
_____

 *poultry*

Recipe Name _____ Serves _____

Ingredients

_____   _____
_____   _____
_____   _____
_____   _____
_____   _____
_____   _____
_____   _____
_____   _____
_____   _____
_____   _____

Method

_____
_____
_____
_____
_____
_____
_____
_____
_____
_____
_____
_____
_____
_____
_____
_____
_____
_____

notes
_____
_____

 *poultry*

Recipe Name _____ Serves _____

Ingredients

_____   _____
_____   _____
_____   _____
_____   _____

Method

_____
_____
_____
_____
_____
_____

notes

_____
_____

poultry

Recipe Name _____ Serves _____

Ingredients

_____   _____
_____   _____
_____   _____
_____   _____

Method

_____
_____
_____
_____
_____
_____

notes

_____
_____

 *poultry*

Recipe Name _____ Serves _____

Ingredients

_____   _____
_____   _____
_____   _____
_____   _____
_____   _____
_____   _____
_____   _____
_____   _____

Method

_____
_____
_____
_____
_____
_____
_____
_____
_____
_____
_____
_____
_____
_____
_____
_____

notes
_____
_____

 *poultry*

Recipe Name _____ Serves _____

Ingredients

_____ _____
_____ _____
_____ _____
_____ _____

Method

_____
_____
_____
_____
_____
_____

notes

_____
_____

poultry

Recipe Name _____ Serves _____

Ingredients

_____ _____
_____ _____
_____ _____

Method

_____
_____
_____
_____
_____

notes

_____
_____
_____

 poultry

Recipe Name _____ Serves _____

Ingredients
_____   _____
_____   _____
_____   _____
_____   _____
_____   _____
_____   _____
_____   _____
_____   _____
_____   _____

Method
_____
_____
_____
_____
_____
_____
_____
_____
_____
_____
_____
_____
_____
_____
_____
_____
_____
_____

notes
_____
_____

 *poultry*

Recipe Name _____ Serves _____

Ingredients

Method

notes

 *poultry*

Recipe Name _____ Serves _____

Ingredients

Method

notes

 *poultry*

Recipe Name _____ Serves _____

Ingredients

_____ _____
_____ _____
_____ _____
_____ _____
_____ _____
_____ _____
_____ _____
_____ _____

Method

_____
_____
_____
_____
_____
_____
_____
_____
_____
_____
_____
_____
_____
_____
_____
_____
_____

notes
_____
_____

 *poultry*

Recipe Name _____ Serves _____

Ingredients

Method

notes

 *poultry*

Recipe Name _____ Serves _____

Ingredients

Method

notes

 *poultry*

Recipe Name _____ Serves _____

Ingredients

_____   _____
_____   _____
_____   _____
_____   _____
_____   _____
_____   _____
_____   _____
_____   _____

Method

_____
_____
_____
_____
_____
_____
_____
_____
_____
_____
_____
_____
_____
_____
_____
_____

notes

_____
_____

 *poultry*

Recipe Name _____ Serves _____

Ingredients

Method

notes

 *poultry*

Recipe Name _____ Serves _____

Ingredients

Method

notes

 *poultry*

Recipe Name _____ Serves _____

Ingredients

_____   _____
_____   _____
_____   _____
_____   _____
_____   _____
_____   _____
_____   _____
_____   _____
_____   _____

Method

_____
_____
_____
_____
_____
_____
_____
_____
_____
_____
_____
_____
_____
_____
_____
_____
_____
_____

notes
_____
_____

Seafood

 seafood

Recipe Name _____ Serves _____

Ingredients

_____   _____
_____   _____
_____   _____
_____   _____
_____   _____
_____   _____
_____   _____
_____   _____
_____   _____

Method

_____
_____
_____
_____
_____
_____
_____
_____
_____
_____
_____
_____
_____
_____
_____

notes
_____
_____

 *seafood*

Recipe Name _____ Serves _____

Ingredients

_____   _____
_____   _____
_____   _____
_____   _____

Method

_____
_____
_____
_____
_____
_____

notes

_____
_____

seafood

Recipe Name _____ Serves _____

Ingredients

_____   _____
_____   _____
_____   _____
_____   _____

Method

_____
_____
_____
_____
_____

notes

_____
_____

 *seafood*

Recipe Name _____ Serves _____

Ingredients

Method

notes

 *seafood*

Recipe Name _____ Serves _____

Ingredients

_____   _____
_____   _____
_____   _____
_____   _____

Method

_____
_____
_____
_____
_____
_____

notes

_____
_____

seafood

Recipe Name _____ Serves _____

Ingredients

_____   _____
_____   _____
_____   _____
_____   _____

Method

_____
_____
_____
_____
_____

notes

_____
_____

seafood

Recipe Name _____ Serves _____

Ingredients

_____   _____
_____   _____
_____   _____
_____   _____
_____   _____
_____   _____
_____   _____
_____   _____

Method

_____
_____
_____
_____
_____
_____
_____
_____
_____
_____
_____
_____
_____
_____
_____
_____
_____

notes
_____
_____

 *seafood*

Recipe Name _____ Serves _____

Ingredients

_____   _____
_____   _____
_____   _____
_____   _____

Method

_____
_____
_____
_____
_____
_____

notes

_____
_____

seafood

Recipe Name _____ Serves _____

Ingredients

_____   _____
_____   _____
_____   _____
_____   _____

Method

_____
_____
_____
_____

notes

_____
_____

 seafood

Recipe Name _____ Serves _____

Ingredients

_____   _____
_____   _____
_____   _____
_____   _____
_____   _____
_____   _____
_____   _____
_____   _____
_____   _____
_____   _____

Method

_____
_____
_____
_____
_____
_____
_____
_____
_____
_____
_____
_____
_____
_____
_____
_____
_____

notes
_____
_____

 *seafood*

Recipe Name _____ Serves _____

Ingredients

_____ _____
_____ _____
_____ _____
_____ _____

Method

_____
_____
_____
_____
_____
_____

_____ *notes* _____
_____
_____

seafood

Recipe Name _____ Serves _____

Ingredients

_____ _____
_____ _____
_____ _____
_____ _____

Method

_____
_____
_____
_____
_____

_____ *notes* _____
_____
_____

 *seafood*

Recipe Name _____ Serves _____

Ingredients

_____   _____
_____   _____
_____   _____
_____   _____
_____   _____
_____   _____
_____   _____
_____   _____
_____   _____
_____   _____
_____   _____

Method

_____
_____
_____
_____
_____
_____
_____
_____
_____
_____
_____
_____
_____
_____
_____
_____
_____
_____

notes

_____
_____

Vegetables
& Sides

vegetables & sides

Recipe Name _____ **Serves** _____

Ingredients

_____   _____
_____   _____
_____   _____
_____   _____
_____   _____
_____   _____
_____   _____
_____   _____

Method

_____
_____
_____
_____
_____
_____
_____
_____
_____
_____
_____
_____
_____
_____
_____

notes
_____
_____

vegetables & sides

Recipe Name _____ Serves _____

Ingredients

_____   _____
_____   _____
_____   _____
_____   _____

Method

_____
_____
_____
_____
_____
_____

notes

_____
_____

vegetables & sides

Recipe Name _____ Serves _____

Ingredients

_____   _____
_____   _____
_____   _____
_____   _____

Method

_____
_____
_____
_____
_____

notes

_____
_____

vegetables & sides

Recipe Name _____ Serves _____

Ingredients

_____   _____
_____   _____
_____   _____
_____   _____
_____   _____
_____   _____
_____   _____
_____   _____

Method

_____
_____
_____
_____
_____
_____
_____
_____
_____
_____
_____
_____
_____
_____
_____

notes
_____
_____

vegetables & sides

Recipe Name _____ Serves _____

Ingredients

_____   _____
_____   _____
_____   _____
_____   _____

Method

_____
_____
_____
_____
_____
_____

_____ *notes* _____
_____
_____

vegetables & sides

Recipe Name _____ Serves _____

Ingredients

_____   _____
_____   _____
_____   _____
_____   _____

Method

_____
_____
_____
_____
_____

_____ *notes* _____
_____
_____

vegetables & sides

Recipe Name _____ Serves _____

Ingredients

_____   _____
_____   _____
_____   _____
_____   _____
_____   _____
_____   _____
_____   _____
_____   _____
_____   _____

Method

_____
_____
_____
_____
_____
_____
_____
_____
_____
_____
_____
_____
_____
_____
_____

notes

_____
_____

vegetables & sides

Recipe Name _____ Serves _____

Ingredients

_____   _____
_____   _____
_____   _____
_____   _____

Method

_____
_____
_____
_____
_____
_____

notes

_____
_____

vegetables & sides

Recipe Name _____ Serves _____

Ingredients

_____   _____
_____   _____
_____   _____
_____   _____

Method

_____
_____
_____
_____

notes

_____
_____

vegetables & sides

Recipe Name _____ Serves _____

Ingredients

_____   _____
_____   _____
_____   _____
_____   _____
_____   _____
_____   _____
_____   _____
_____   _____

Method

_____
_____
_____
_____
_____
_____
_____
_____
_____
_____
_____
_____
_____
_____
_____
_____
_____
_____

notes
_____
_____

vegetables & sides

Recipe Name _____ Serves _____

Ingredients

_____   _____
_____   _____
_____   _____
_____   _____

Method

_____
_____
_____
_____
_____

notes
_____
_____

vegetables & sides

Recipe Name _____ Serves _____

Ingredients

_____   _____
_____   _____
_____   _____

Method

_____
_____
_____
_____
_____

notes
_____
_____

# vegetables & sides

Recipe Name _____ Serves _____

Ingredients

_____   _____
_____   _____
_____   _____
_____   _____
_____   _____
_____   _____
_____   _____
_____   _____

Method

_____
_____
_____
_____
_____
_____
_____
_____
_____
_____
_____
_____
_____
_____
_____
_____

notes
_____
_____

vegetables & sides

Recipe Name _____ Serves _____

Ingredients

_____   _____
_____   _____
_____   _____
_____   _____

Method

_____
_____
_____
_____
_____

notes

_____
_____

vegetables & sides

Recipe Name _____ Serves _____

Ingredients

_____   _____
_____   _____
_____   _____

Method

_____
_____
_____
_____

notes

_____
_____

vegetables & sides

Recipe Name _____ Serves _____

Ingredients

_____   _____
_____   _____
_____   _____
_____   _____
_____   _____
_____   _____
_____   _____
_____   _____
_____   _____

Method

_____
_____
_____
_____
_____
_____
_____
_____
_____
_____
_____
_____
_____
_____
_____
_____
_____

notes

_____
_____

Breads
& Breakfast

breads & breakfast

Recipe Name _____ Serves _____

Ingredients

Method

notes

Recipe Name _____ Serves _____

Ingredients

_____ _____

_____ _____

_____ _____

_____ _____

Method

_____

_____

_____

_____

_____

_____

notes

_____

_____

breads & breakfast

Recipe Name _____ Serves _____

Ingredients

_____ _____

_____ _____

_____ _____

Method

_____

_____

_____

_____

notes

_____

_____

_____

breads & breakfast

Recipe Name _____ Serves _____

Ingredients

Method

notes

breads & breakfast

Recipe Name _____ Serves _____

Ingredients

_____   _____
_____   _____
_____   _____
_____   _____

Method

_____
_____
_____
_____
_____
_____

notes

_____
_____

breads & breakfast

Recipe Name _____ Serves _____

Ingredients

_____   _____
_____   _____
_____   _____
_____   _____

Method

_____
_____
_____
_____
_____

notes

_____
_____

breads & breakfast

Recipe Name _____ Serves _____

Ingredients

_____   _____
_____   _____
_____   _____
_____   _____
_____   _____
_____   _____
_____   _____
_____   _____

Method

_____
_____
_____
_____
_____
_____
_____
_____
_____
_____
_____
_____
_____
_____
_____

notes
_____
_____

breads & breakfast

Recipe Name _____ Serves _____

Ingredients

_____ _____
_____ _____
_____ _____
_____ _____

Method

_____
_____
_____
_____
_____
_____
_____

notes
_____
_____
_____

breads & breakfast

Recipe Name _____ Serves _____

Ingredients

_____ _____
_____ _____
_____ _____
_____ _____

Method

_____
_____
_____
_____
_____
_____

notes
_____
_____
_____

breads & breakfast

Recipe Name _____ Serves _____

Ingredients

Method

notes

breads & breakfast

Recipe Name _____ Serves _____

Ingredients

_____   _____
_____   _____
_____   _____

Method

_____
_____
_____
_____
_____
_____

notes

_____
_____

breads & breakfast

Recipe Name _____ Serves _____

Ingredients

_____   _____
_____   _____
_____   _____

Method

_____
_____
_____
_____

notes

_____
_____

breads & breakfast

Recipe Name _____ Serves _____

Ingredients

_____   _____
_____   _____
_____   _____
_____   _____
_____   _____
_____   _____
_____   _____
_____   _____

Method

_____
_____
_____
_____
_____
_____
_____
_____
_____
_____
_____
_____
_____
_____
_____
_____

notes
_____
_____

Desserts

 *desserts*

Recipe Name _____ Serves _____

Ingredients

_____   _____
_____   _____
_____   _____
_____   _____
_____   _____
_____   _____
_____   _____
_____   _____
_____   _____

Method

_____
_____
_____
_____
_____
_____
_____
_____
_____
_____
_____
_____
_____
_____
_____
_____

notes
_____
_____

 *desserts*

Recipe Name _____ Serves _____

Ingredients

_____   _____
_____   _____
_____   _____
_____   _____

Method

_____
_____
_____
_____
_____
_____

notes

_____
_____

desserts

Recipe Name _____ Serves _____

Ingredients

_____   _____
_____   _____
_____   _____
_____   _____

Method

_____
_____
_____
_____
_____

notes

_____
_____

 *desserts*

Recipe Name _____ Serves _____

Ingredients

_____   _____
_____   _____
_____   _____
_____   _____
_____   _____
_____   _____
_____   _____
_____   _____
_____   _____

Method

_____
_____
_____
_____
_____
_____
_____
_____
_____
_____
_____
_____
_____
_____
_____
_____
_____

notes
_____
_____

 *desserts*

Recipe Name _____ Serves _____

Ingredients

_____   _____
_____   _____
_____   _____
_____   _____

Method

_____
_____
_____
_____
_____

notes

_____
_____

desserts

Recipe Name _____ Serves _____

Ingredients

_____   _____
_____   _____
_____   _____
_____   _____

Method

_____
_____
_____
_____

notes

_____
_____

 *desserts*

Recipe Name _____ Serves _____

Ingredients

_____ _____
_____ _____
_____ _____
_____ _____
_____ _____
_____ _____
_____ _____
_____ _____

Method

_____
_____
_____
_____
_____
_____
_____
_____
_____
_____
_____
_____
_____
_____
_____
_____
_____
_____

notes
_____
_____

 *desserts*

Recipe Name _____ Serves _____

Ingredients

_____   _____
_____   _____
_____   _____
_____   _____

Method

_____
_____
_____
_____
_____
_____

notes

_____
_____

desserts

Recipe Name _____ Serves _____

Ingredients

_____   _____
_____   _____
_____   _____

Method

_____
_____
_____

notes

_____
_____

 desserts

Recipe Name _____ Serves _____

Ingredients

_____   _____
_____   _____
_____   _____
_____   _____
_____   _____
_____   _____
_____   _____
_____   _____
_____   _____

Method

_____
_____
_____
_____
_____
_____
_____
_____
_____
_____
_____
_____
_____
_____
_____
_____
_____

notes
_____
_____

 *desserts*

Recipe Name _____ Serves _____

Ingredients

Method

notes

desserts

Recipe Name _____ Serves _____

Ingredients

Method

notes

 *desserts*

Recipe Name _____ Serves _____

Ingredients

Method

notes

 *desserts*

Recipe Name _____ Serves _____

Ingredients

_____   _____
_____   _____
_____   _____
_____   _____

Method

_____
_____
_____
_____
_____
_____

notes

_____
_____

desserts

Recipe Name _____ Serves _____

Ingredients

_____   _____
_____   _____
_____   _____
_____   _____

Method

_____
_____
_____
_____
_____

notes

_____
_____

 desserts

Recipe Name _____ Serves _____

Ingredients

_____   _____
_____   _____
_____   _____
_____   _____
_____   _____
_____   _____
_____   _____
_____   _____
_____   _____

Method

_____
_____
_____
_____
_____
_____
_____
_____
_____
_____
_____
_____
_____
_____
_____
_____

notes _____
_____

 *desserts*

Recipe Name _____ Serves _____

Ingredients

_____   _____
_____   _____
_____   _____
_____   _____

Method

_____
_____
_____
_____
_____
_____

notes

_____
_____

desserts

Recipe Name _____ Serves _____

Ingredients

_____   _____
_____   _____
_____   _____
_____   _____

Method

_____
_____
_____
_____
_____

notes

_____
_____

 desserts

Recipe Name _____ Serves _____

Ingredients

Method

notes

 *desserts*

Recipe Name _____ Serves _____

Ingredients

_____ _____
_____ _____
_____ _____
_____ _____

Method

_____
_____
_____
_____
_____
_____

notes

_____
_____

desserts

Recipe Name _____ Serves _____

Ingredients

_____ _____
_____ _____
_____ _____

Method

_____
_____
_____
_____
_____

notes

_____
_____

 desserts

Recipe Name _____ **Serves** _____

Ingredients

_____ _____
_____ _____
_____ _____
_____ _____
_____ _____
_____ _____
_____ _____
_____ _____
_____ _____

Method

_____
_____
_____
_____
_____
_____
_____
_____
_____
_____
_____
_____
_____
_____
_____

notes
_____
_____

 *desserts*

Recipe Name _____ Serves _____

Ingredients

_____   _____
_____   _____
_____   _____
_____   _____

Method

_____
_____
_____
_____
_____
_____

notes

_____
_____

desserts

Recipe Name _____ Serves _____

Ingredients

_____   _____
_____   _____
_____   _____
_____   _____

Method

_____
_____
_____
_____
_____

notes

_____
_____

Basic Substitutions

If the recipe calls for   **You can substitute:**

Flour:

1 cup sifted all-purpose flour . . . . .1 cup less 2 tablespoons unsifted all-purpose flour
1 cup sifted cake flour . . . . .1 cup less 2 tablespoons sifted all-purpose flour
1 cup sifted self-rising flour . . . . .1 cup sifted all-purpose flour plus 1½ teaspoons
                                                baking powder and a pinch of salt

Milk/Cream:

1 cup buttermilk . . . . .1 cup plain yogurt, or 1 tablespoon lemon juice or
                                                vinegar plus enough milk to measure 1 cup—let stand
                                                for 5 minutes before using
1 cup whipping cream or half-and-half . . . . .⅞ cup whole milk plus 1½ tablespoons butter
1 cup light cream . . . . .⅞ cup whole milk plus 3 tablespoons butter
1 cup sour cream . . . . .1 cup plain yogurt
1 cup whole milk . . . . .1 cup skim or nonfat milk plus 2 tablespoons butter
                                                or margarine

Seasonings:

1 teaspoon allspice . . . . .½ teaspoon cinnamon plus ⅛ teaspoon cloves
1 cup ketchup . . . . .1 cup tomato sauce plus ½ cup sugar plus
                                                2 tablespoons vinegar
1 teaspoon Italian spice . . . . .¼ teaspoon each oregano, basil, thyme, rosemary
                                                plus a dash of cayenne pepper
1 teaspoon lemon juice . . . . .½ teaspoon vinegar

Sugar:

1 cup confectioners' sugar . . . . .½ cup plus 1 tablespoon granulated sugar
1 cup granulated sugar . . . . .1¾ cups confectioners' sugar, 1 cup packed
                                                light brown sugar, or ¾ cup honey

Other:

1 package active dry yeast . . . . .½ cake compressed yeast
1 teaspoon baking powder . . . . .¼ teaspoon cream of tartar plus ¼ teaspoon
                                                baking soda
1 cup dry bread crumbs . . . . .¾ cup cracker crumbs or 1 cup cornflake crumbs
1 cup (2 sticks) butter . . . . .⅞ cup vegetable oil or 1 cup (2 sticks) margarine
1 tablespoon cornstarch . . . . .2 tablespoons all-purpose flour
1 cup dark corn syrup . . . . .¾ cup light corn syrup plus ¼ cup light molasses
1 cup light corn syrup . . . . .1 cup maple syrup
1⅔ ounces semisweet chocolate . . . . .1 ounce unsweetened chocolate plus 4 teaspoons
                                                granulated sugar
1 ounce unsweetened chocolate . . . . .3 tablespoons unsweetened baking cocoa plus
                                                1 tablespoon butter or margarine
1 (1-ounce) square chocolate . . . . .¼ cup baking cocoa plus 1 teaspoon shortening
1 cup honey . . . . .1 to 1¼ cups sugar plus ¼ cup liquid, or
                                                1 cup corn syrup or molasses
1 egg . . . . .¼ cup mayonnaise

Charts

Equivalents

When the recipe calls for   **Use**

Baking
½ cup (1 stick) butter . . . . .4 ounces
2 cups (4 sticks) butter . . . . .1 pound
4 cups all-purpose flour . . . . .1 pound
4½ cups sifted cake flour .1 pound
1 square chocolate . . . . .1 ounce
1 cup semisweet chocolate chips . . . . .6 ounces
2¼ cups packed brown sugar . . . . .1 pound
4 cups confectioners' sugar . . . . .1 pound
2 cups granulated sugar . . . . .1 pound

Cereal/Bread
1 cup fine dry bread crumbs. . . . . 4 to 5 slices
1 cup soft bread crumbs . . . . 2 slices
1 cup fine saltine crumbs. . . . . 28 saltines
1 cup fine graham cracker crumbs. . . . . 15 graham crackers
1 cup crushed cornflakes. . . . . 3 cups uncrushed
4 cups cooked macaroni . . . . 8 ounces uncooked
3½ cups cooked rice. . . . . 1 cup uncooked

Dairy
1 cup shredded cheese . . . . .4 ounces
1 cup cottage cheese . . . . .8 ounces
1 cup sour cream . . . . .8 ounces
1 cup whipped cream . . . . .½ cup heavy cream
⅔ cup evaporated milk . . . . .1 (5⅓-ounce) can
1⅔ cups evaporated milk . . . . .1 (13-ounce) can

Fruit
4 cups sliced or chopped apples . . . . .4 medium
1 cup mashed bananas . . . . .3 medium
2½ cups shredded coconut .8 ounces
3 to 4 tablespoons lemon juice . . . . .1 lemon
⅓ cup orange juice . . . . .1 orange
3 cups raisins . . . . .1 (15-ounce) package

Freezer Storage

Wrap food in airtight, moisture- and vapor-proof material to prevent odors from penetrating the freezer and foods. List the date on all items before placing them in the freezer. When defrosting frozen foods, allow enough time to do so in the refrigerator. You can refreeze partially thawed food if it still has ice crystals in it, except shellfish and vegetables. If food has been at 40 degrees or higher, do not refreeze.

Freezer Storage of Common Foods

Foods	Average freezer life
Breads	2 to 3 months
Butter or margarine	4 to 6 months
Cakes (baked and unfrosted)	2 to 6 months
Cheese	3 to 4 months
Beef roasts and steaks	6 to 12 months
Ground beef	3 to 4 months
Pork roast	4 to 6 months
Pork chops	3 to 4 months
Ham	2 months
Bacon	1 month
Whole chicken	3 to 6 months
Chicken pieces	3 months
Cooked chicken	1 month
Turkey	6 months
Fish	2 to 3 months
Lobster, scallops, or crab	1 to 2 months
Other shellfish	3 to 4 months
Frozen fruits (commercially packaged)	1 year
Frozen vegetables (commercially packaged)	8 months

To freeze fresh vegetables, blanch by briefly submerging in boiling water, and then immediately submerge in cold water for 4 to 5 minutes.

Foods Not Suitable for Freezing

Bananas	Onions	Tomatoes
Cabbage	Pears	Hard-cooked eggs
Celery	Processed meats	Cucumbers
Radishes	Mayonnaise	Salad greens

Recipe Finder

Appetizers

Recipe Name	Cookbook	Page

Breads & Breakfast

Recipe Name	Cookbook	Page

Recipe Finder

Desserts

	Recipe Name	Cookbook	Page

Meats

	Recipe Name	Cookbook	Page

Recipe Finder

Meats	Recipe Name	Cookbook	Page

Poultry	Recipe Name	Cookbook	Page

Salads	Recipe Name	Cookbook	Page

Recipe Finder

Seafood	Recipe Name	Cookbook	Page

Soups	Recipe Name	Cookbook	Page

Vegetables & Sides	Recipe Name	Cookbook	Page

Index

Index

Index

Index

FRP™